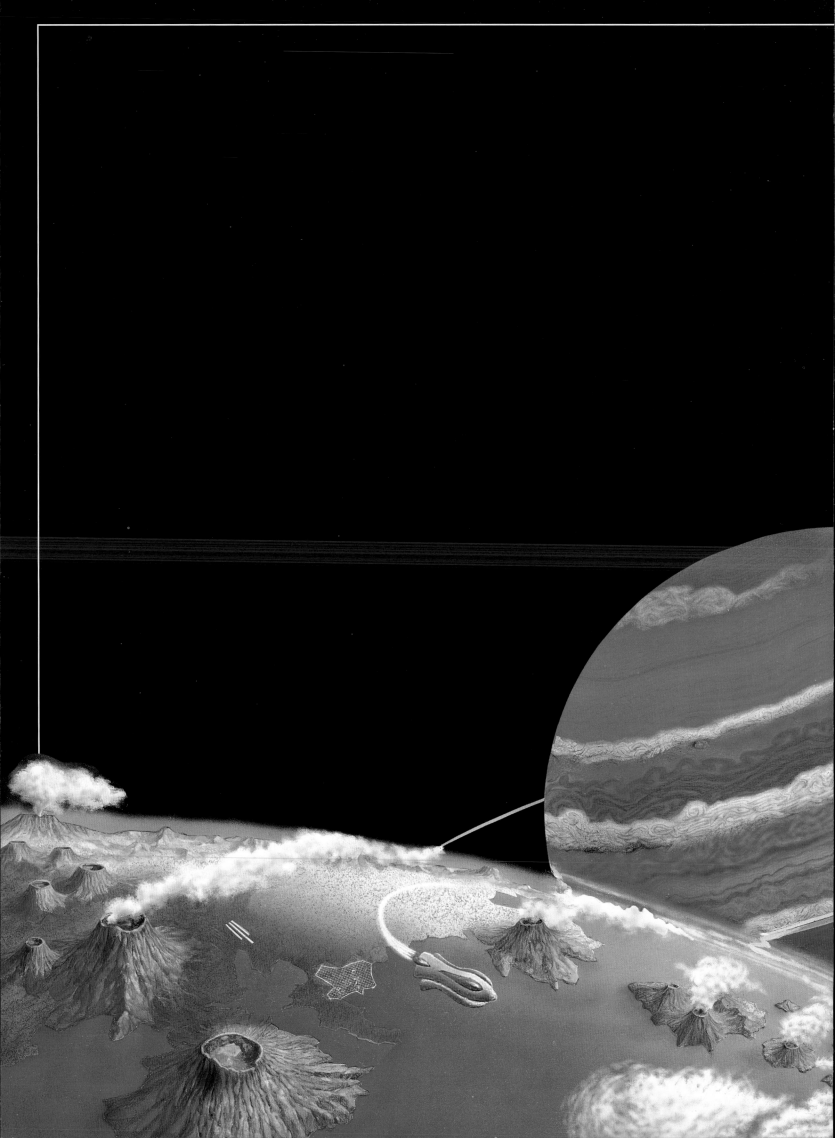

Is Anybody Out There?

Heather Couper and Nigel Henbest

Illustrated by Luciano Corbella

DK PUBLISHING, INC.

A DK PUBLISHING BOOK

Editors	Lorrie Mack
	Jackie Wilson
US Editors	Kristin Ward
	Nicole Zarick
Art Editor	Martyn Foote
Managing Editor	Anna Kruger
Senior Managing Art Editor	Peter Bailey
DTP Designer	Andrew O'Brien
Production	Charlotte Traill
	Josie Alabaster
Picture Researcher	Liz Moore

First American Edition, 1998

2 4 6 8 10 9 7 5 3 1

Published in the United States by
DK Publishing, Inc.
95 Madison Avenue, New York, New York 10016

Visit us on the World Wide Web at http://www.dk.com

Library of Congress Cataloging-in-Publication Data

Couper, Heather.
Is anybody out there? : the search for life beyond our planet /
Heather Couper & Nigel Henbest : illustrated by Luciano Corbella.
p.   cm.
Includes index.
Summary: Explores the possibility of life on other planets from both scientific and mythological perspectives.
ISBN 0-7894-2798-2
1. Life on other planets–Juvenile literature. [1. Life on other planets.] I. Henbest, Nigel. II. Corbella, Luciano,ill.
III. Title.
QB54.C68   1998
576.8'39–dc21
                                                    97-35398
                                                        CIP
                                                        AC

Reproduced by Colourscan, Singapore
Printed in Italy by L.E.G.O.

Contents

Is this what they look like?

ALIENS. THEY LEAP OUT FROM THE PAGES of science fiction magazines, invade our homes through the TV set, and become stars on the big screen. But do they really exist? Until recently, most scientists would not even consider the possibility of alien life. Now we know so much about our place in the Universe that the alien question won't go away. Earth is an ordinary planet, circling an average star; if life happened here, then why not elsewhere? But one thing's certain, alien life won't look anything like the aliens portrayed in movies. In many cases, their humanoid appearance owes more to limited film and TV budgets than it does to the way biology would evolve in a truly alien world.

As well as imagining aliens, writers and artists dream of the future of planet Earth. In the magazine story "Cities in the Air" (1929), New York rises above pollution on an antigravity cushion.

Flash Gordon (1936)
Faced with an enemy like this, the fearless Flash Gordon could hardly know if he was battling aliens or a troop of Teutonic soldiers.

Man From Planet X (1951)
A twist to the usual idea of alien visitation, this film featured an extraterrestrial visitor whose intentions were genuinely friendly. However, the humans were anything but.

The Day the Earth Stood Still (1951)
An alien and his robot land on Earth to protest nuclear testing. He is similar enough to us to disguise himself as a human.

Zombies of the Stratosphere (1952)
Aliens again visit Earth in vaguely humanoid shapes, including a Martian who saves the Earth from devastation.

Invaders from Mars (1953)
Aside from its hands and eyes, this alien – here capturing and brainwashing the inhabitants of a small town – could pass for human.

Flash Gordon (1940)
This later alien, capturing Dale Arden, may have a suitably extraterrestrial head, but still a remarkably humanoid body.

Them (1954)
While appearing to be the most alien creature on this page, ironically this monster is merely a terrestrial ant mutated by leakages of radiation from nuclear tests.

One of a series of cartoons published in the *New York Times* in 1835 depicting views of aliens on the Moon, allegedly obtained through a telescope in South Africa.

Aliens in history

Many astronomers in the 17th and 18th centuries imagined that all the planets were inhabited by beings who, like us, took pleasure in food, music, and art. The 17th-century Dutch scientist Christiaan Huygens, who discovered Saturn's rings, suggested that Jupiter and Saturn were ideal worlds for sailors because they have so many moons to assist navigation. Other astronomers even believed that life could exist on the Sun! With increasing knowledge, those beliefs waned, only to return with a vengeance in the late 19th century, when the Martian "canals" were discovered. Were these built by intelligent Martians to irrigate a planet that was drying out? For the first time, the notion of alien life gripped the imagination of the public, and the fascination has never gone away.

Close Encounters of the Third Kind (1977)
One of Steven Spielberg's early successes, this movie turned fear of an alien invasion into joy at their coming. The shots of the pedestal-shaped Devil's Tower in Wyoming – the focus for the UFO activity – are haunting.

Superman (1978)
Superman, the most popular superhero, was an alien baby sent to Earth for safety before his own planet, Krypton, exploded.

Star Trek (1979)
The movie and TV series were more concerned with social and environmental messages than with the science of alien life – hence the humanoid aliens who often speak perfect English!

This Island Earth (1954)
These aliens abduct Earth scientists to save their own planet. They may have strange hands and feet, but the size and shape of their bodies is rather familiar.

Invasion of the Star Creatures (1962)
They may have come from the stars, but the marauders have evolved in a manner remarkably similar to us, even down to their kneecaps!

Invaders from Mars (1986)
When the film was remade 30 years later, audiences expected invading Martians to look less human.

Spaced Invaders (1990)
A gang of Martians invades the Earth on Halloween. With figures and costumes like this, they didn't look out of place!

The birth of life

OUR SEARCH FOR INTELLIGENT LIFE in the Universe must begin at home. Planet Earth is the only place where we know life exists. From its volcanic beginnings, the young Earth spawned the first microscopic living cells that evolved, over billions of years, into a rich variety of plants and animals. If we can understand how life on Earth was created from rocks, gas, and water, then we can start to surmise whether alien life may have arisen on other planets.

Violent beginnings

Some scientists believe the raw material for life was the gas spewing from volcanoes: simple molecules in the gas were welded into larger, more complex molecules by energy from lightning and possibly sunlight.

LIFE, CARBON, AND ORGANIC MOLECULES

Carbon atoms are the basis of all life, as they combine with each other and other atoms to make complex and versatile compounds. Such carbon compounds were first found in living cells, so chemists call them "organic." Astronomers have now found carbon-rich "organic molecules" in the Universe that have *not* been produced by life. They are often black and are like coal or tar.

1 CHOKING "AIR"

Volcanic gases cloaked early Earth in a dense, choking atmosphere of water vapor, carbon dioxide, and nitrogen, with some methane, hydrogen, and ammonia. Split by lightning, these molecules regrouped as complex organic compounds, such as amino acids.

Atmosphere's ingredients

2 ATMOSPHERIC CHANGES

Water vapor condensed into a planet-wide rainstorm lasting millions of years. Most of the organic molecules created by lightning were washed into the oceans, leaving an "air" of carbon dioxide and nitrogen, similar to that of present-day Venus and Mars.

| 4,600 mya | 4,000 mya | 3,000 mya | 2,000 mya |

Over three billion years ago, organic molecules joined together to create the first forms of life. They were very simple creatures consisting of a single cell, rather like algae, bacteria, or amoebas.

THE ORIGINS OF LIFE

In 1953, American chemist Stanley Miller (b.1930) put a mixture of gases — simulating Earth's early atmosphere — in a flask, and passed electric sparks through it overnight to mimic lightning. Water in the flask represented the early ocean. In the morning, Miller found the transparent gases had turned to an orange-brown "gunk" dissolved in the water. The experiment had created several new and complex compounds, including amino acids.

Stanley Miller – the first scientist to experiment with the origin of life.

PRIMORDIAL SOUP

The organic molecules made in the atmosphere were washed into the oceans, forming a thin "primordial soup." In rock pools, the soup became concentrated and the amino acids joined to make proteins. Other molecules reacted to build deoxyribonucleic acid (DNA) while fatty molecules formed a protective membrane that surrounded everything. The first living cells were born.

These Australian stromatolites — giant colonies of single cells — show how the first life on Earth may have looked.

Inside the cell

All life on Earth – animal, plant, or microbe – is made from the same types of organic molecules, containing some of the most common elements in the Universe: carbon, hydrogen, oxygen, and nitrogen. They are packaged into microscopic cells that all work in a surprisingly similar way. The different parts of the cell probably started as "minicells," which teamed up to work more effectively.

The human body is made up of 50 billion cells. Skin cells, nerve cells, and muscle cells are all similar inside.

Plant cells contain green chlorophyll, for turning carbon dioxide into oxygen. Otherwise, they are similar to animal cells.

Mitochondrion

Ribosome

DNA

MITOCHONDRION
The mitochondrion is the cell's powerhouse; it creates energy by "burning" sugar in oxygen. Instead of producing a flame, a slow-motion reaction releases a continual stream of energy-packed molecules that deliver power where it's needed.

RIBOSOME
The ribosome is the factory; it assembles the small "building-block" molecules, amino acids, into proteins. Some proteins form the cell's structures; others, called enzymes, control the reactions that keep the cell functioning.

NUCLEUS
The nucleus contains the long double helix of DNA, which holds the chemical information for everything the cell does.

REPRODUCTION
When a cell divides, the inherited DNA ensures that the "daughter cells" are identical to the parent.

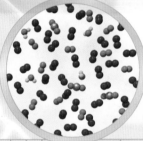

3 TURNING THE TABLES
Over the next 2 billion years, evolving plants turned most of the carbon dioxide into oxygen. Then the life that was created from atmospheric gases changed that atmosphere to suit its own requirements.

4 UNIQUE ATMOSPHERE
Life created an atmosphere, unique in the Solar System, of mainly nitrogen and oxygen. In the upper atmosphere, oxygen atoms formed the ozone layer, protecting the surface from the Sun's lethal rays.

1,000 mya

500 mya

Time in millions of years ago (mya)

Ancestor of fish

Ozone layer allowed life to flourish on land.

EARLY TRIALS
The early cells eventually learned to work together to build complex plants and animals. Earth's oceans were alive with a weird collection of biological experiments 570 million years ago. Most did not survive; but one or two became the ancestors of the fish.

ON TO LAND
Some fish evolved into amphibians, moving from the protective ocean to land now screened by the ozone layer. With them went some seaweeds, which eventually became grass, trees, and flowers. A number of amphibians evolved into reptiles, dinosaurs, birds, mammals, and eventually humans.

Impact!

L IFE IN THE UNIVERSE is constantly under threat from bombardment. In its early days, Earth was pounded by rocky or metallic asteroids and frozen comets – debris left over from the building of the Sun and planets. But this apparent threat to emerging life was actually a blessing in disguise. By wiping out weak forms of life, bombardment encouraged the evolution of stronger, more versatile strains. Some scientists now believe that most of Earth's water and the other raw materials of life did not come from volcanoes but were dumped on our planet from space.

Comets: bringers of life?

Comets have long been associated with doom and destruction. In the past, when comets were less understood, the appearance of a comet in the sky – a ghostly dagger poised to strike – must have been terrifying. But spaceprobes, such as *Giotto*, have revealed that comets could be bringers of life, because they contain vast quantities of organic molecules and water. In its distant home, far from the Sun, a comet is a frozen lump of ice and rock a few miles across. But as it plummets toward the heat of the Sun, its evaporating gases expand into a huge head of steam, swept away by the solar wind into a glowing tail millions of miles long.

Comets striking Earth were more common in the distant past when "construction site" debris was more plentiful. Today, major impacts occur at roughly 100 million year intervals.

Comets in their natural state mostly reside in the Oort Cloud, a huge, spherical reservoir of millions of frozen bodies possibly stretching halfway to the nearest stars.

Europe's Giotto *probe skimmed past Halley's Comet in 1986. It revealed jets of gas spewing out of an icy lump 6 miles (10 km) across and coated, to astronomers' surprise, in dark, organic "tar."*

FRED — THE MAVERICK

Sir Fred Hoyle, although a brilliant scientist, can hardly be described as conventional. One of his ideas is that life arrived fully formed – possibly even hatched – in "eggs" that were brought to Earth in comets. Another is that the dark, sooty "dust" that collects together into huge clouds in space is in fact freeze-dried bacteria that cause mass Earth epidemics, such as AIDS and flu.

British astronomer Fred Hoyle (b.1915) is primarily famous for his "Steady State" theory, which holds that the Universe has no beginning and no end.

A cornucopia of organic molecules is frozen into an icy comet. Comets may have "seeded" the Earth with these raw materials for life.

Once a comet becomes trapped in a close orbit around the Sun, it steadily boils away. After about 250,000 years, it is reduced to tiny grains of dust.

Young Earth – and presumably other planets – were blitzed by cosmic impacts that delivered water and dark patches of organic molecules.

COSMIC RUBBLE

The gap between the orbits of Mars and Jupiter is littered with thousands of lumps of rock and metal, called asteroids. The strong gravity of Jupiter stops the asteroids from assembling into a planet.

What wiped out the dinosaurs?

The dinosaurs – that had ruled Earth for over 100 million years – became extinct 65 million years ago, along with many other species. At the same time, rocks worldwide were enriched with vast quantities of the element iridium, which is rare on our planet but common in comets and asteroids. It is thought that an object 6 miles (10 km) across smashed into Yucatan in Mexico, where there is now a large crater. The huge explosion sent up a pall of iridium-rich dust, blotting out the Sun for months. Plant life was devastated, and few animals survived.

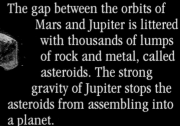

Dinosaurs might have been wiped out by a cosmic impact, one of several that are thought to have caused mass extinctions.

One in the eye for Jupiter

In March 1993, the veteran American comet-hunting team of Carolyn and Gene Shoemaker and David Levy discovered a comet near Jupiter. Unusually, it looked like a string of pearls. Astronomers were astonished to discover that it had been pulled apart into more than 20 pieces by Jupiter's enormous gravity. They were even more amazed to find that Comet Shoemaker-Levy 9 was on a collision course with the planet. In July 1994, the fragments rammed into Jupiter at 135,000 mph (216,000 km/h), producing colossal explosions.

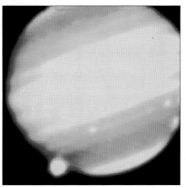

Infrared (heat) image of one of the 1994 impacts: some of the comet's fragments were 2.5 miles (4 km) across.

The aftermath, imaged by the *Hubble Space Telescope*: the impact left "black eyes" of organic molecules.

SPACEGUARD!

Although most asteroids live beyond Mars, some – maybe as many as 2,000 – have orbits that bring them close to Earth. One day an asteroid like this could hit us, and astronomers are busy tracking them down. The international "Project Spaceguard" would be activated if an asteroid was bent on collision. By exploding a nuclear warhead nearby, the asteroid would be pushed off course.

Nuclear warheads

Exploding warhead alters course of approaching asteroid.

On the trail of Martians

PLANET MARS IS THE NEAREST plausible home for alien life. Rumors of intelligent Martians began in the 19th century with sightings of "canals" on Mars and have been stoked by incidents such as Orson Welles's terrifyingly real radio play in 1939, "reporting" a Martian invasion of Earth! The latest surge of optimism came with the possible discovery of fossils from Mars (pages 16–17). But the "ups" have been balanced by deep "downs." The first spaceprobe images of the planet showed a barren and lifeless world, and astronomers' hopes were dashed.

Bombarded planet

As late as the 1950s, astronomers were hopeful that some primitive plant life, such as mosses or lichens, might live on Mars. But the first spaceprobe pictures were bitterly disappointing. They revealed an almost airless world – heavily pockmarked with impact craters – that looked more like the Moon than the Earth. But the probes had been surveying just one hemisphere of the planet; it later emerged that Mars has a far more interesting side.

Mars's barren, cratered surface was first revealed by NASA's *Mariner 4* spaceprobe in 1965.

Panorama of present-day Martian landscape.

HUNTING DOWN THE MARTIANS

In 1877, Italian astronomer Giovanni Schiaparelli reported seeing long, straight lines on Mars. He called them "canali" (Italian for channels). But American amateur astronomer Percival Lowell, a rich Boston businessman, mistranslated this as "canals" (deliberately constructed watercourses). Mars was drying out, he maintained, and intelligent Martians living on the equator had built the canals to bring water from the polar caps in an attempt to save their world.

Mars-obsessed Lowell built a large observatory in Arizona dedicated to observing the planet.

The canals turned out to be optical illusions, caused by the eye's tendency to "see" geometrical shapes in faint detail. Spaceprobe images show no trace of them.

VIKING: IN SEARCH OF LIFE

In 1971, *Mariner 9* saw Mars's other side. The first probe to orbit the Red Planet, it revealed a hemisphere in which giant volcanoes and colossal chasms combined to produce one of the most dramatic – and Earthlike – landscapes in the Solar System. But most important of all, *Mariner 9* discovered traces of dried river beds. If there had ever been water on Mars, then life might have started. These discoveries spurred NASA to build two *Viking* craft – the first spaceprobes to be sent to another planet in search of life. Each craft consisted of an *Orbiter* and a *Lander*.

Both Landers touched down safely in Mars's northern hemisphere in mid-1976. Some 4,010 miles (6,460 km) apart, they were almost on opposite sides of the planet.

Mars's soil is red because it's rusty – a result of the water that flowed in the past.

The long arm scooped up soil to be analyzed within the Lander.

Robot laboratory

The *Viking* scientists thought the Martian soil might contain microscopic cells, resembling bacteria or yeast. To check for life, each *Lander* carried out four experiments in a laboratory the size of a large wastepaper basket. The results show reactive chemicals in the soil – but no life.

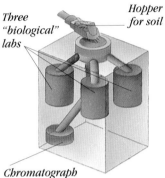

Three "biological" labs

Hopper for soil

Chromatograph separates elements.

FORENSIC SCIENCE

Like a police lab analyzing traces from a crime, the gas chromatograph broke down the soil into its basic atoms. It detected many chemical elements, including iron, silicon, and oxygen. But there was no sign of carbon, the basic building block of life.

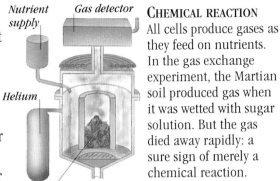

Nutrient supply *Gas detector*

Helium

Soil wetted with sugar produces gas.

CHEMICAL REACTION

All cells produce gases as they feed on nutrients. In the gas exchange experiment, the Martian soil produced gas when it was wetted with sugar solution. But the gas died away rapidly: a sure sign of merely a chemical reaction.

FERMENTATION

In the labeled release experiment, any yeast present would generate gases as they do in fermenting wine. Gas did pour off, but production soon stopped, indicating a chemical reaction.

Gas detector

Nutrient supply

Gas produced for a short time only

COOKING

A bright lamp in the pyrolytic release experiment encouraged any plantlike cells to grow and multiply. After five days, the soil was heated, and a detector "sniffed out" any aromas from freshly cooked cells. The results were inconclusive.

Artificial sun

"Cooking aromas" broken down to simple gases

Gas detector

Heat breaks down the chemicals in the soil.

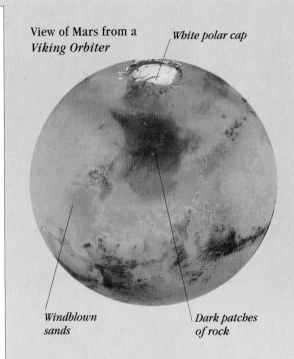

View of Mars from a Viking Orbiter *White polar cap*

Windblown sands

Dark patches of rock

Mars: the sterile world

Mars today appears to be a lifeless world. The shifting dark markings, once thought to be growing vegetation, are now known to be areas of rocks periodically covered and uncovered by windblown sands. The water that was once plentiful on the planet is now frozen into the soil as permafrost; and the white polar caps are made largely of frozen carbon dioxide. Most telling of all, Mars now has a planetwide ozone hole. It allows ultraviolet radiation from the Sun to penetrate all the way to the surface — sterilizing the soil and destroying any living cells that might once have evolved here.

The antenna sent signals to the Viking Orbiter, *busy mapping the planet from high above, which relayed them to Earth.*

A meteorology boom checked out wind speed and air temperature.

Particles of red soil, suspended in the thin air, tinge Mars's sky salmon-pink.

Two cameras provided stereoscopic views.

ROBOT ON THE RED PLANET

The two *Viking Landers* were the most sophisticated spaceprobes ever built. Each was a truly intelligent robot, with stereoscopic color vision, chemistry and biology laboratories, a weather station, and a communications dish.

Mars: abode of life?

ALTHOUGH BARREN NOW, Mars was a very different world in the past. Close-up scrutiny by spaceprobes has revealed evidence that Mars once had tumbling streams and a substantial atmosphere. Billions of years ago, volcanoes and Mars-quakes made the planet far more active and it was a lot warmer. Scientists have even proposed that there may have been shallow oceans. In these conditions – similar to those prevailing on the young Earth – life may well have got started.

Mars attacks!

Young Mars was a violent place. Volcanoes rumbled and Mars-quakes shook the ground. Together with the abundant water and thick atmosphere, all the ingredients were present for the creation of life. Even frequent comet and meteorite impacts supplied fresh materials. But in the end, this rain of bombardment may have ended the chance of life by blasting away most of the atmosphere of this small, low-gravity planet.

HERE'S LOOKIN' AT YOU

The "Face on Mars" has been described as a huge artifact from a lost Martian civilization, like a vast Egyptian pyramid. However, seen from a different perspective, as in this computer-generated image (below left), the 1 mile (1.5 km)-long "face" shows itself for what it is: a naturally wind-eroded hill, one of several in the vicinity.

The wind-eroded hill shows up on this computer-generated image.

Bombardments may have helped create life, but on Mars they may have also destroyed it.

The same panorama as seen on pages 14–15, but 3 billion years earlier. Young Mars resembled early Earth, with active volcanoes and fast-flowing rivers.

Volcanic eruptions and impacts of icy comets provided water for the rivers that once flowed across Mars's surface.

The Martians have landed!

In August 1996, NASA scientists caused a worldwide sensation when they announced that tiny structures found in a meteorite blasted out of Mars might be fossils of primitive life. The fossils were estimated to be 3.6 billion years old. But when the excitement died down, other scientists examined the evidence and concluded that the "fossils" were more likely to be of mineral, rather than animal, origin.

MESSENGER FROM MARS

ALH84001 — the rock from Mars — landed in Antarctica 13,000 years ago and was preserved in an ice sheet. It is one of 12 Martian meteorites currently under investigation.

MARTIAN CREEPY-CRAWLY?

Magnified 100,000 times, these bacterium-shaped "fossils" discovered in ALH84001 are one-hundredth the diameter of a human hair.

Mars Pathfinder braked its entry into the Martian atmosphere with a heat-resistant aeroshell.

On reaching the lower layers of the atmosphere, it deployed a huge parachute.

NASA's Global Surveyor kept a watch on Mars from orbit.

Japan's Planet-B will study Mars's upper atmosphere.

Mars — the search continues

After a lull of more than 20 years — when there were no successful missions to Mars — a veritable flotilla of spaceprobes was targeted toward the Red Planet in the late 1990s. First in the race were NASA's *Mars Pathfinder* and *Global Surveyor*. They will be followed by a series of American, Russian-European, and Japanese spacecrafts. These will drop penetrators to pierce deep into the soil and deploy balloons and rovers to comb the entire Martian surface for signs of life.

On landing, protective "petals" unfolded to reveal the scientific instruments.

Mars Pathfinder landed in an ancient flood-channel littered with huge boulders once carried by raging torrents of water.

Artist's impression of first Mars base

There's now little doubt that the next destination for the human race is Mars. Some experts believe that the first crewed mission will take place before 2020. Within 100 years of this landing, the first Martian bases will be built.

Mars Pathfinder carried the first robot rover to another planet — named "Sojourner" (traveler) after Sojourner Truth (1797–1883), a freed slave who spoke out for women's rights.

Mars's volcanoes may have been active until only a few million years ago.

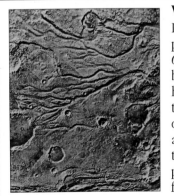

VANISHED RIVERS

Long, curved channels photographed by the *Viking Orbiters* look like dried river-beds. These water courses must have been an impressive sight in the planet's youth. Some were over 75 miles (100 km) wide, a result of flash floods. But as the atmosphere ebbed away, the planet grew colder and the water froze into the soil as permafrost.

Fish on Jupiter?

THE OBVIOUS PLACE TO SEARCH FOR LIFE in the Solar System may be Mars, but there are other possibilities. Some planets can be ruled out entirely: Mercury and Venus are too hot; Uranus, Neptune, and Pluto are too cold. But Jupiter and Saturn, along with their vast families of moons, may just have a chance. After all, life exists in some pretty extreme environments on Earth. Attention currently focuses on Jupiter's moons, which are warmer than they should be this far from the Sun because they are "pummeled" by Jupiter's gravity.

Waterworld?

Dazzlingly white and smooth as a billiard ball, Europa is unlike any other moon in the Solar System. Close-up images from NASA's *Galileo* spaceprobe suggest it is covered in shifting ice floes, like arctic pack ice. Some scientists believe that an ocean lies below, warmed by eruptions from undersea volcanoes. Earth has similar thermal vents on the ocean floor and exotic creatures live around them. In his novel *2010*, British science fiction author Arthur C. Clarke imagined life forms on Europa. He may have been prophetically accurate.

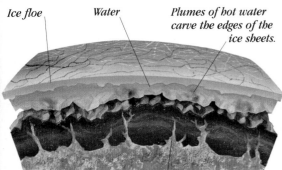

Ice floe   *Water*   *Plumes of hot water carve the edges of the ice sheets.*

Under Europa's icy surface, a huge ocean may be home to life that thrives on volcanic heat instead of sunlight.

Heat from the core rises through thermal vents ("undersea volcanoes") to heat the water.

By Jove!

Jupiter is by far the biggest planet in the Solar System – so large that all the other planets, or 1,300 Earths, could fit inside it. Unlike the inner planets, such as Earth or Mars, it is made almost completely of gases, including organic molecules such as methane and acetylene. In the center is a small rocky core, heated by the weight of the overlying layers to 63,000°F (35,000°C), and so Jupiter is warmer than would be expected at 483 million miles (778 million km) from the Sun. The planet is surrounded by 16 moons, four of which – Io, Europa, Ganymede, and Callisto – are similar in size to the planets Mercury and Pluto.

CALLISTO

Valhalla

Callisto is the most heavily cratered of all Jupiter's moons, with one crater – Valhalla – measuring 185 miles (300 km) across. It looks like Earth's Moon but is made of ice.

DISTANT DRUMS

While spaceprobes hunt for life on, or in, our planetary neighbors, many scientists believe we will first be alerted to alien life by radio signals from much farther away. As the foldout pages underneath this page reveal, there's even a way of calculating how many advanced civilizations "out there" may be broadcasting to us.

Europa

The smooth, icy surface may conceal a huge, warm ocean.

Jupiter is stripy because of its rapid spin (it rotates in about 10 hours). The white "zones" are ice crystals high in its atmosphere; the colored belts may be colored by organic compounds.

Saturn's Titanic mystery

Titan, at 3,200 miles (5,150 km) across, is Saturn's largest moon. It is the only moon in the Solar System with a thick atmosphere, composed mainly of nitrogen, like Earth's air. *Voyager 1*, specially targeted to fly close by in 1980, could see nothing through impenetrable cloud cover, but it did confirm the presence of methane. Scientists have speculated that Titan might be like "an early Earth in deep freeze," with organic molecules frozen on its surface. If warmed by a nearby volcano, perhaps they could combine to make life.

Titan's orange clouds, seen here from *Voyager 1*, are probably made of oily, organic droplets.

GANYMEDE

Ganymede, 3,270 miles (5,260 km) across, is the biggest moon in the Solar System. Although probably too cold for life, the *Galileo* probe has detected organic molecules on its surface.

Ganymede's ancient gnarled surface reveals a history of impacts and geological activity.

Io is the most active moon in the Solar System, with still-erupting volcanoes that create local hotspots of up to 2,725°F (1,500°C) on its surface.

IO

Wracked by volcanic eruptions, Io's surface is forever changing. It is heated internally by the pull of Jupiter's gravity, causing plumes of sulfur to shoot 185 miles (300 km) into space.

The Great Red Spot is a storm big enough to swallow three Earths. The red color is due to phosphorus, an element essential to living organisms.

PIERCING THE VEIL

In 2004, the *Cassini* spaceprobe will arrive at Saturn. Its subprobe, *Huygens*, will plunge into Titan's clouds and image the surface. Scientists believe it will find a world with lakes of liquid methane and ethane — like natural gas on Earth — with rich accumulations of organic molecules, and mountains that may be active volcanoes. There's a faint chance that primitive bacteria might have evolved in the warmth of the volcanic vents.

JUPITER-FISH

The American astronomer Carl Sagan (page 42) suggested that Jupiter's clouds might be populated by "Jupiter-fish." These hypothetical creatures inhale gas through their front ends and exhale it through their rear ends, thereby propelling themselves along. The tongue-in-cheek suggestion was intended to open up people's minds to the potential diversity of life in the Universe.

Large, slow-moving grazers, as big as Iceland

Smaller, faster hunters

Have they visited us?

L IFE ELSEWHERE IN OUR SOLAR SYSTEM – if it exists at all – would be merely "green slime" – certainly nothing we would want to communicate with. But could there be life in solar systems beyond our own? Many people think so. Some even believe that there are civilizations so advanced that they can build starships to conquer the vast gulfs of space, and that these aliens have not only visited Earth, but left evidence behind to prove it. On this spread are some of the most persuasive examples of alien visitations, from ancient lines in the deserts of Peru to UFO sightings. But on investigation, the evidence for them being alien always breaks down.

California-based mystic George Adamski caused a sensation in the 1950s when he claimed to have been abducted to Venus in a flying saucer. On close inspection, it turned out to be made of chicken feeders and bottle coolers.

Aliens in history

Believers in alien visitations maintain that there is a great deal of archaeological and historical evidence to back their claim that Earth has been the focus of numerous extra-terrestrial landings. They point to the sophistication of the pyramids in Egypt and Mexico, the complexity of the Nazca Lines in Peru, and the sheer scale of the Easter Island statues – primitive people, they argue, could never have managed such gargantuan feats. And they comb the Bible for passages that could be interpreted as alien sightings, or even the aftermath of a nuclear explosion. But there are equally valid down-to-Earth explanations for all these strange phenomena.

An ancient cave painting in Italy of a figure with domed headgear. However, it is more likely to be an ancient headdress than a space helmet, as some claim.

Old rock paintings from the Nazca Plains in Peru contain figures that are claimed to represent aliens – there is also a close resemblance to the traditional costume in that area.

STATUES FROM OUTER SPACE

Some people maintain that the statues on Easter Island are so massive that they could only have been carved, then raised, by aliens using advanced technology. But Thor Heyerdahl, a Norwegian anthropologist, restaged their construction using local people and old stone tools. He concluded that each statue would take a year to build – well within the power of human beings.

The Pyramids of Giza are aligned precisely north-south, with interior passages pointing toward the stars of Orion. But this is an indication of long-established human intelligence, rather than alien visitors.

Flying saucers

In the summer of 1947, US pilot Kenneth Arnold was amazed to see nine silvery disks skimming at nearly 1,250 mph (2,000 km/h) over the Cascade Mountains in Washington State. A reporter nicknamed them "flying saucers." Since then, there have been thousands of sightings of "unidentified flying objects" (UFOs). But despite considerable investigation, there is still no explanation of what they might be.

Almost certainly, the vast majority of UFOs are natural phenomena – meteors or even ball lightning – that are misinterpreted. This metallic-looking object photographed by Paul Trent in 1950 over his farm in Oregon remains inexplicable, but there is no evidence that it came from another planet.

CROP CIRCLES

Every summer since the late 1980s, flattened circles and other geometrical shapes have suddenly appeared in cornfields all over Britain. Some people believe they are the landing sites of flying saucers. But they could equally well be the result of summer-time revels by students or young farmers.

Over the years, crop circles have been growing more complex – a testimony to the skill of their human creators!

NAZCA LINES

The Nazca Desert in southern Peru is criss-crossed with a bewildering pattern of lines and geometrical shapes so enormous that they only make sense when seen from the air. Were they, as some claim, runways for UFOs? Probably not: UFOs would have got stuck in the soft sand. The lines are probably of religious origin, designed so that the gods of the sky would notice the people below. The Nazca Lines were made by removing stones from the desert to reveal the lighter subsoil.

EGYPTIAN PYRAMIDS

The Great Pyramids at Giza are built on such a majestic scale that some believe their construction was the work of visiting aliens. But the Egyptian civilization dates back to 5,000 BC. Archaeologists have now established that pyramid construction techniques evolved over the millennia, leading to the magnificent examples that have survived to this day.

In the Bible, Ezekiel describes the appearance in the sky of a fiery object with whirling wheels that spoke to him.

ALIENS IN THE BIBLE

The many accounts of visitations by angels in the Bible are sometimes interpreted as alien sightings. Even the destruction of Sodom and Gomorrah is said to have been caused by a nuclear explosion, which turned Lot's wife into a pillar of salt! But the best-attested case of a UFO sighting in the Bible is in Ezekiel. His UFO was probably a series of parhelia, or "sundogs" – bright images of the Sun refracted by high-level clouds.

NEW WORLD PYRAMIDS

The pyramids of Mexico and the carvings within them are sometimes interpreted as the work of an alien civilization. The carvings are compared to images of astronauts driving spacecraft, and the pyramids lauded as engineering miracles way ahead of their time. But the carvings are simply intricate religious imagery, and the pyramids are elaborate stone cairns used to bury the dead.

Worlds beyond

To TRACK DOWN INTELLIGENT LIFE means reaching out beyond our Solar System. In particular, it involves finding planets around other stars: sites where life could develop. But even the nearest stars are a million times farther away than our Sun – and while planets are small and dark, stars are big and bright. So the task is like looking for moths circling streetlights in New York from the distance of London. But in the past few years, astronomers have developed more sensitive equipment, and are confident that they have located at least a dozen "extrasolar" planets. So far only massive planets – as heavy as Jupiter – have been found; planets like the Earth may also be there, but are too lightweight to be detected with current techniques.

It takes all types

Planetary systems are thought to be born in a swirling disk of gas and dust, and astronomers once assumed that they would all look like our Solar System – with small planets close in and larger ones farther out. The newly discovered systems look anything but.

Beta Pictoris, with its disk of debris, may be too young to have formed planets yet.

Didier Queloz and Michel Mayor: first to discover an extrasolar planet.

NEW WORLDS

On October 6, 1995, Michel Mayor and Didier Queloz of the Geneva Observatory in Switzerland, announced that they had discovered a planet orbiting the sunlike star 51 Pegasi. Three months later, Geoff Marcy and Paul Butler found planets circling two more stars, 47 Ursae Majoris and 70 Virginis.

PULLING POWER

The number of extrasolar planets now known exceeds the number of planets in the Solar System, but no one has actually seen them. These worlds have been pinpointed because of their gravitational pull on their parent stars – and to detect this, the planets must be massive.

Paul Butler and Geoff Marcy have evidence for the existence of at least eight extrasolar planets.

The right stuff

The sunlike star, 47 Ursae Majoris – 35 light-years away, in the constellation of the Great Bear – was found by American astronomers Geoff Marcy and Paul Butler to have a planet weighing in at 2.3 times the mass of Jupiter. It lies at twice the distance from its star as the Earth does from the Sun – where it may still be warm enough for liquid water to exist and for life to develop. If, as in our Solar System, giant planets are surrounded by extensive retinues of moons, life might have started on one of these as well.

Planet of 47 Ursae Majoris

A moon circling the planet belonging to 47 Ursae Majoris could have volcanoes, water, plants, and intelligent life.

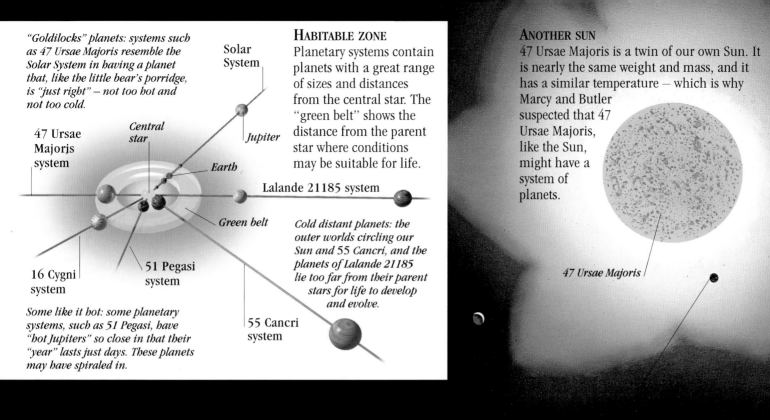

"Goldilocks" planets: systems such as 47 Ursae Majoris resemble the Solar System in having a planet that, like the little bear's porridge, is "just right" – not too hot and not too cold.

Solar System

47 Ursae Majoris system

Central star

Jupiter

Earth

47 Ursae Majoris system

Green belt

16 Cygni system

51 Pegasi system

55 Cancri system

Some like it hot: some planetary systems, such as 51 Pegasi, have "hot Jupiters" so close in that their "year" lasts just days. These planets may have spiraled in.

HABITABLE ZONE

Planetary systems contain planets with a great range of sizes and distances from the central star. The "green belt" shows the distance from the parent star where conditions may be suitable for life.

Lalande 21185 system

Cold distant planets: the outer worlds circling our Sun and 55 Cancri, and the planets of Lalande 21185 lie too far from their parent stars for life to develop and evolve.

ANOTHER SUN

47 Ursae Majoris is a twin of our own Sun. It is nearly the same weight and mass, and it has a similar temperature – which is why Marcy and Butler suspected that 47 Ursae Majoris, like the Sun, might have a system of planets.

47 Ursae Majoris

GAS GIANT OR SLIME WORLD?

The planet orbiting 47 Ursae Majoris might be a gas giant like Jupiter, possibly with huge floating life-forms (see page 19). Or its dense atmosphere might overlie a solid surface, coated with slime that has dripped from its clouds under the influence of its powerful gravity.

47 Ursae Majoris's known planet is a little farther from its star than Mars is from the Sun. Smaller planets, as yet undetected, may circle closer in.

Bands of swirling gases

Vast hurricane

Rings around the planet are the remains of a moon smashed to pieces by a striking comet.

Planet hunting

Extrasolar planets are too dim to be seen directly, so astronomers track them down by investigating stars that are behaving oddly. As a planet orbits its parent star, its gravity pulls the star, causing it to sway slightly. This wobble can be detected by two techniques.

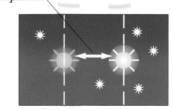

Orbit of star

Center of gravity

A star and its planet circle their mutual center of gravity.

Orbit of planet

A swaying star indicates an unseen planet.

FOLLOW THAT STAR

Astronomers, using powerful telescopes, can detect a star being swung from side to side by planets too faint to see. This method works best for far-out planets, and needs years of observation to follow one orbit.

Wavelengths of light

Star's spectrum

Dark lines shift toward blue.

Dark lines shift toward red.

SEEING THE LIGHT

Astronomers split the star's light into a spectrum. As the star is swung toward us, its lightwaves are compressed and the dark lines in the spectrum shift toward blue; as the star is swung away, the dark lines shift toward red.

What a difference 10g makes

I F LIFE HAS EVOLVED on any of the newly discovered planets in our Galaxy, what would it look like? All life-forms, no matter how alien, would share some characteristics: eyes, ears, mouth, and reproductive organs, for instance. But the position of these organs would not necessarily bear any resemblance to the human layout. Environment, too, has a part to play. Creatures would evolve differently on the small world "Moo," where the pull of gravity (0.1g) is only one-tenth of Earth's, and on the giant planet "Peg," where the gravity is 10g.

THE ALTERNATIVE HUMAN

You might have looked like this! "Arnold" was designed by a biologist to show how life might have evolved on Earth if different creatures had gained the upper hand 570 million years ago (see page 11). The environment that led to Arnold was identical to the conditions that gave rise to humans.

Arnold has three eyes on stalks, three arms (one a thick but sensitive feeler), and three legs.

The world Moo

Moo is a moon circling the giant planet Peg (the worlds seen on the previous spread). Because it is small, it has low gravity. Except at star-rise and star-set, it is also cold, because its star spends a good deal of time eclipsed behind giant Peg. But life-forms on Moo have adapted to these conditions. They grow high, curl up when cold, have big eyes to see in the dark, and have developed efficient ways of breathing in the thin air.

Moo-man stands with his gills stretched, enjoying the warmth of star-rise.

Moo-creatures breathe through huge branching gills – the air is so thin, that breathing passages and lungs are useless.

A set of large eyes opens in dim light, while a circlet of compound eyes gives all-around vision in bright light.

They "speak" by rubbing their tentacles together. Their mouths are just above the ground, close to the plants they feed on.

Moo-woman curls protectively around her new offspring, budded from the end of a tentacle. When it matures, the offspring will separate to lead an independent existence.

Moo-creatures reproduce sexually, by interlocking specialized tentacles.

Star-rise in the 47 Ursae Majoris system. The star is about to pass behind the planet Peg, leaving Moo dark and cold.

DAILY ECLIPSE

With its thin air, the sky above Moo always looks dark: you can easily see the faint glowing atmosphere of its parent star 47 Ursae Majoris. Soon after star-rise, the star will disappear behind the giant planet Peg, and Moo will be enveloped in a long eclipse until the star emerges shortly before star-set.

Moo's plant life is purple, because it photosynthesizes a different form of chlorophyll.

Water is essential to life on Moo. Strange as they look, the creatures on Moo are made of water – the universal solvent – and organic compounds that are rather similar to the ingredients of life on Earth.

The watery oceans on Moo would be familiar to us.

The planet Peg

Peg is a giant world with high gravity and a dense, choking atmosphere. But underneath, it has a sludgy surface populated by millions of Peg-creatures. They are very different from the inhabitants of Moo. The 10g gravity and intense pressure makes them very flat, and they are sightless – the thick atmosphere is so foggy that eyes are useless. Instead, Peg-creatures establish their whereabouts by using sonar, like bats on Earth.

To withstand the pressure, the Peg-creatures are massively fortified, like submersibles that descend to the bottom of Earth's deepest oceans.

Hornlike apertures on the back emit sonar pulses for location.

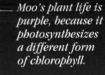

A slitlike mouth scoops up the sludgy soil and sifts it for microorganisms to eat.

Massive paddlelike legs propel the creatures across the slimy surface.

The body features protrude very little. The creatures are also very sluggish, so that they don't overheat.

The fish on Moo are a familiar shape, because the form of their bodies is dictated by the buoyancy of the water rather than gravity.

Talking alien

ALIENS WILL CERTAINLY look very different from us, and think differently, too. And, unlike movie aliens, they won't speak fluent English — so how are we ever going to communicate with them? Phil Morrison, an American physicist and expert on extra-terrestrial life, believes that aliens would communicate in codes designed to be broken as easily as possible. Here are some of our own attempts to send easily decipherable messages from Earth to the stars.

Arecibo's message with the 1,679 pulses rearranged in 73 rows of 23 columns to form a pictogram.

Message to M13

In 1974, astronomers at Arecibo in Puerto Rico sent a message from humankind to the stars. Lasting just three minutes, it was a signal consisting of 1,679 on-off pulses beamed toward M13, a dense ball of a million stars lying 25,000 light-years away. An intelligent alien living there would realize that 1,679 is the product of two prime numbers, 23 and 73. Arranging the pulses into a rectangle 23 columns wide and 73 rows deep creates a pictogram explaining the basis of life on Earth.

If, in 25,000 years, someone in M13 receives the Arecibo message, we'll have to wait 25,000 years for the reply.

The wavy lines represent the radio waves beaming the signal from Arecibo into space. The peaks and troughs are separated by a wavelength of 5 in (12.6 cm.)

PIONEERING MESSAGE

The first spaceprobes to leave the Solar System, *Pioneer 10* and *11*, both carried engraved plaques explaining who had sent them — the cosmic equivalent of the "message in a bottle." The plaques revealed the whereabouts of the Earth, the position of the Solar System, and the outlines of a man and a woman.

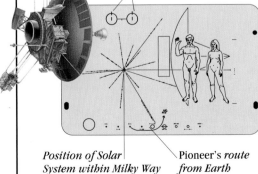

Hydrogen atoms — the most common element in space.

Position of Solar System within Milky Way

Pioneer's route from Earth

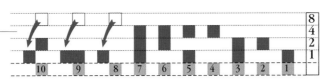

Voyaging to the stars

The two starward-bound *Voyager* spacecraft, which flew past Jupiter and Saturn between 1979 and 1981, also carry a message. It's an old-fashioned LP record, complete with a stylus to enable the aliens to play it!

THINK OF A NUMBER
The first block shows, from right to left, the numbers 1 to 10 in binary code – the form computers use.

15-Phosphorus

1-Hydrogen

8-Oxygen

7-Nitrogen

6-Carbon

ELEMENTS OF LIFE
This block picks out five numbers: they are the atomic numbers (number of protons) of the most important elements of life.

MAGIC MOLECULES
These blocks reveal the proportions of the five key elements in certain molecules – sugar (C_5H_7O coded green), phosphate (purple), and the nucleotides (orange) – making up the structure of DNA.

C_5H_7O

C_5H_7O

THE DOUBLE HELIX
The two twisted strands show the "double helix" structure of DNA, the huge molecule that divides and replicates to pass on the "blueprint" of life.

IN A HUMAN IMAGE
The outline of a human – probably the most baffling image to an alien – is flanked by the world's population (left) and the human's height (right).

Height of a human: 14 wavelengths of the signal

Earth *Sun*

Solar System with Earth's location indicated.

SELF-PORTRAIT OF THE SENDER
The last image shows an outline of the radio telescope at Arecibo, with a sketch of how the radio waves were beamed.

THE SOUNDS OF EARTH
The *Voyager* disk is encoded with sounds and pictures that attempt to encapsulate life on Earth. There are greetings in 56 languages (including whale-speak); sounds from a frog-croak to thunder; 90 minutes of music ranging from tribal chants to a Beethoven string quartet; and 118 coded pictures. It will be another 40,000 years before the *Voyagers* speed past their first nearby stars – but the record should last a billion years.

The LP record is made of copper, but gold-plated for protection.

When decoded, one image shows the 200 meter final at the 1972 Munich Olympics. Will the aliens realize this symbolizes the human competitive spirit?

Postcard of a crowded planet: NASA decided that another fitting image of Earth was a packed street scene taken in Lahore, Pakistan.

Talk to the animals

Humans share the Earth with at least two other intelligent species: primates (apes and monkeys) and cetaceans (dolphins and porpoises). Communicating with these species is good practice for speaking alien: but how easy is it?

Dolphins can use a variety of sounds to "name" different objects.

A suspended platform houses transmitters and receivers at the telescope's focus.

EARTH STATION
At 1,000 feet (305 meters) across, the Arecibo radio telescope is the biggest in the world – a bowl of fine wire mesh spanning a natural limestone hollow in Puerto Rico. It spends most of the time "listening in" rather than beaming out, investigating natural sources of radio waves, such as gas clouds, pulsars, and distant galaxies.

Chimps can communicate with humans using signs.

ALIENS ON EARTH
Chimps and dolphins can follow instructions such as "put red brick on top of green" and "swim through hoop." Dolphins can apply a word like "through" to a new situation – for example, "swim through pipe" – and chimps can produce sentences to ask for a banana. These species can use our language, but there is little evidence that they *understand* it. And we do not comprehend the language they use.

The search begins

THE EMERGING SCIENCE of radio astronomy in the 1950s saw the start of the search for extraterrestrial intelligence (SETI). Scientists speculated that aliens could use radio waves for interstellar communication, just as we use them to transmit radio and TV programs on Earth. Unlike expensive and energy-hungry spacecraft, radio waves are cheap, can zip across huge gulfs of space at the speed of light, and can be targeted exactly where needed.

COMMUNICATING WITH FIRE, MIRRORS, AND FORESTS

Attempting to contact aliens is not a new idea. In the 19th century, a number of well-respected scientific figures came up with plans to advertise our existence that seem bizarre today. One advocated digging huge geometrically shaped trenches in the Sahara desert, filling them with oil, and setting fire to them. Another suggested erecting a network of mirrors across Europe in the shape of the stars of the Plow, and using them to beam sunlight to Mars. In 1820, the German mathematician Karl Gauss proposed cutting Siberian forests to form square-shaped stands of trees surrounding a huge triangle to demonstrate the Pythagorean theorem. Due to lack of money, none of the schemes came into operation.

Huge, square-shaped forests surrounding a triangle would tell aliens that there was intelligent life on Earth.

Project Cyclops would have involved an array of 1,500 radio telescopes packed in a circle of 10 miles (16 km) in diameter, scanning the skies for signals from extraterrestrial sources.

FRANK DRAKE — FATHER OF SETI

In the 1950s, when a young American, Frank Drake, was working in the brand new field of radio astronomy, aliens were something no respectable scientist thought about. But Drake took a much broader view. Radio dishes, he knew, could pick up naturally produced signals from halfway across the Universe. They could also be used, in reverse, to transmit a signal. He wondered if there were other intelligences out there using telescopes to transmit messages that his instruments should be able to pick up.

Frank Drake devised the "Drake equation" – a formula to calculate how many civilizations might be broadcasting radio signals (pages 20–23).

A cyclopean endeavor

By the early 1970s, astronomer Frank Drake had attracted an enthusiastic band of SETI researchers around him. They began to devise ingenious schemes to eavesdrop on aliens – the most grandiose of which was Project Cyclops (named after the Greek giant with one eye). The "eye" would have consisted of 1,500 huge radio telescopes crowded onto a circular site. But with a price tag equivalent to $50 billion in today's money, it never got off the drawing board.

"Big Ear" bounced radio waves from space off two giant reflectors to focus the radio waves at ground level.

Radio waves — from space

Focused signal

Reflector curved to focus radio waves

Reflector tilted to point to different regions of the sky

The "Wow!" signal

All SETI researchers have experienced the heartstopping moment when they think they have detected an alien signal. The most dramatic moment of all came in August 1977, when the Ohio State University's radio telescope – nicknamed "Big Ear" – picked up the strongest unidentified signal ever. Seeing the strength of the signal on the paper chart pouring out in the control room, a researcher scrawled "Wow!" in the margin. But it never returned; like many other transient signals detected, it was almost certainly terrestrial – most likely from a military satellite.

Paul Horowitz with META: it sifts through so much radio interference that he calls it "the biggest garbage can in the world."

MEGABUCKS FOR ET

Following the success of the movie *ET* in 1982, the director, Steven Spielberg, offered $100,000 to help SETI track down the real ET. With the cash, Paul Horowitz, a professor of physics at Harvard, built the Megachannel Extraterrestrial Assay (META) – a set of computer chips which, when attached to a radio telescope, could tune in to 8 million extraterrestrial "radio stations" simultaneously. META has been joined by BETA – the Billion-Channel Extra-terrestrial Assay. There have been false alarms, but Horowitz has not yet detected a definite alien signal.

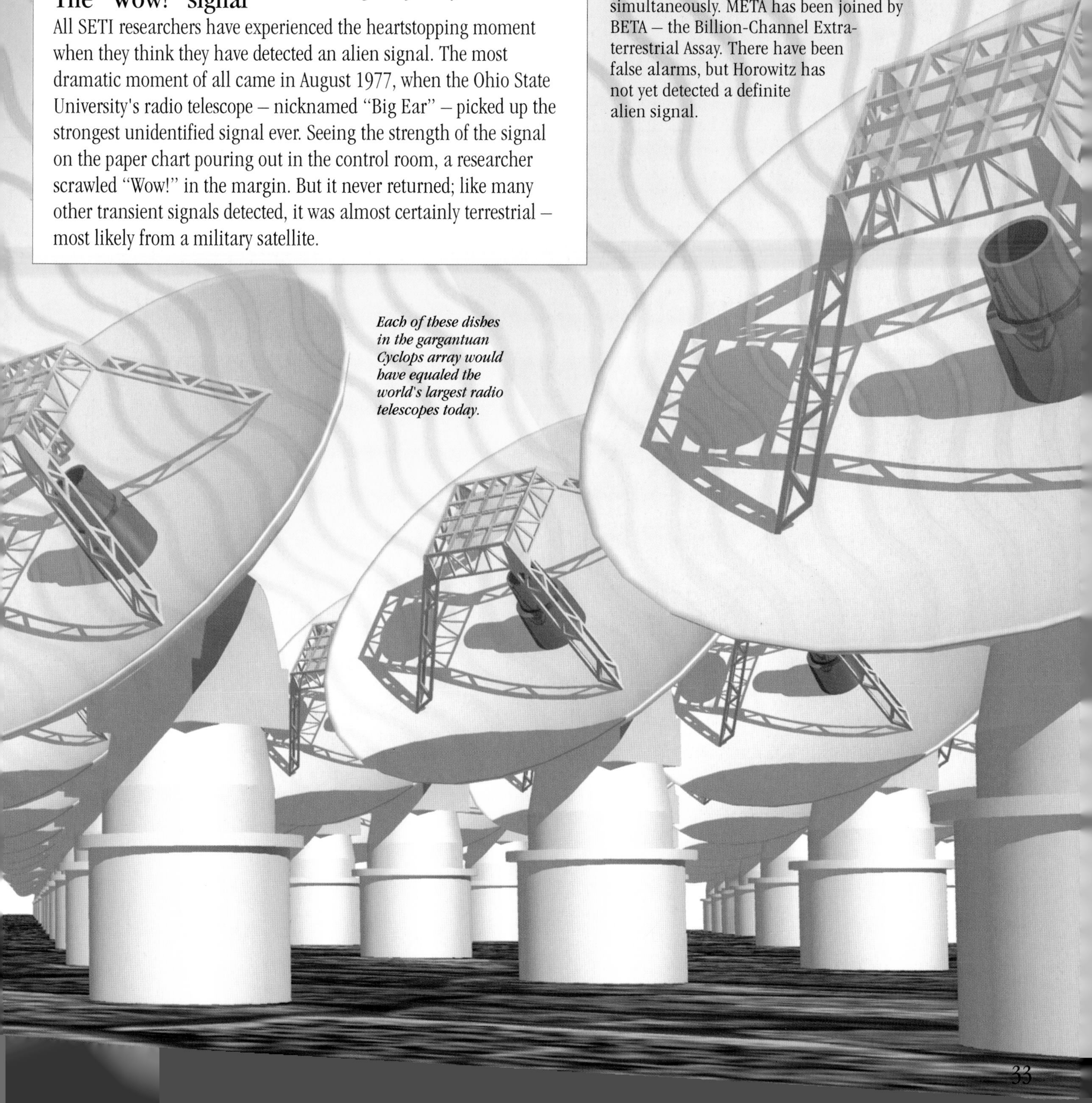

Each of these dishes in the gargantuan Cyclops array would have equaled the world's largest radio telescopes today.

ET: please phone Earth!

TODAY, THE SEARCH FOR EXTRATERRESTRIAL INTELLIGENCE (SETI) is considered by most scientists to be a respectable area of research. However, as recently as 1993, US senators canceled a $100 million SETI project funded by NASA, deriding it as a "great Martian chase." But now the researchers are back in action with Project Phoenix. Every minute of every day, someone somewhere on Earth is searching for signs of alien intelligence.

OAK RIDGE
A few miles outside Boston, Paul Horowitz (p 33) uses this 85-ft (26-m) telescope for his BETA and META projects. It was first used by Frank Drake.

GOLDSTONE
This dish, in the Mojave Desert in California, was used in NASA's canceled SETI program to scan the whole sky.

We've got you covered

SETI has gone worldwide. The map shows locations where searches have been carried out, although not all are still active. SETI researchers now use all kinds of instruments.

RADIO TELESCOPE
Radio telescopes are still the most efficient SETI tools, because radio waves – which travel almost unimpeded through space – provide an ideal way to communicate.

OPTICAL TELESCOPE
Optical telescopes (and other detectors of shorter wavelength radiation, such as ultraviolet and infrared) are used in searches for unusual signals or alien structures.

HAT CREEK
California

LEUSCHNER
California

MOUNT WILSON
California

MOUNT LEMMON
Arizona

VERY LARGE ARRAY
New Mexico

ALGONQUIN
Ontario

COLUMBUS
Ohio

HAYSTACK
Massachusetts

FIVE COLLEGE
Massachusetts

GREENBANK
West Virginia

ARECIBO
Puerto Rico

NORTH AMERICA

SOUTH AMERICA

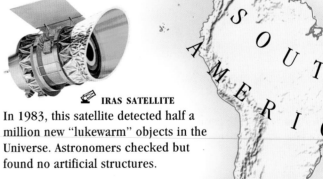

IRAS SATELLITE
In 1983, this satellite detected half a million new "lukewarm" objects in the Universe. Astronomers checked but found no artificial structures.

JILL TARTER
Jill Tarter, of the SETI Institute in California, is probably the most experienced SETI researcher in the world. She followed her degree in engineering physics with research into astrophysics, before combining her two areas of expertise to devise SETI programs. She currently runs Project Phoenix.

KENT CULLERS
Kent Cullers, also of the SETI Institute, is a computer genius. Although blind since birth, he devises the pattern recognition software that will enable researchers to detect an alien signal in a sea of radio noise.

PARQUE PEREYRA IRAOLA
Argentinean astronomers run BETA and META programs on this radio telescope near Buenos Aires.

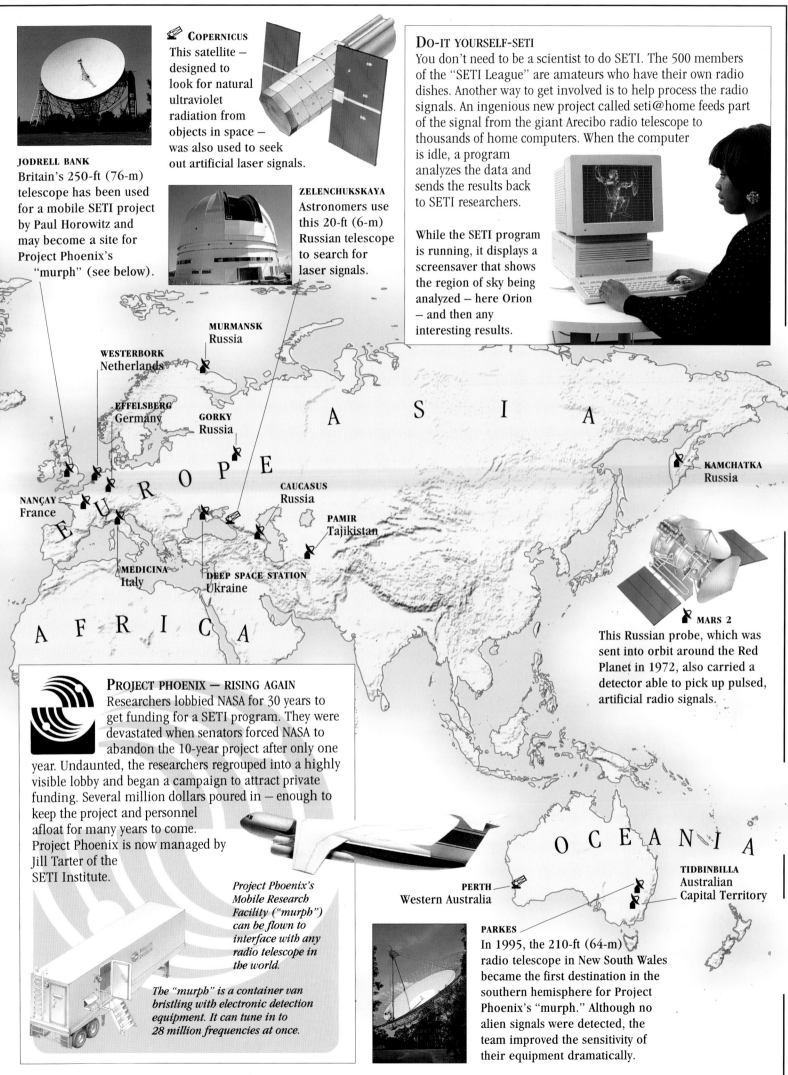

COPERNICUS
This satellite — designed to look for natural ultraviolet radiation from objects in space — was also used to seek out artificial laser signals.

JODRELL BANK
Britain's 250-ft (76-m) telescope has been used for a mobile SETI project by Paul Horowitz and may become a site for Project Phoenix's "murph" (see below).

ZELENCHUKSKAYA
Astronomers use this 20-ft (6-m) Russian telescope to search for laser signals.

DO-IT YOURSELF-SETI
You don't need to be a scientist to do SETI. The 500 members of the "SETI League" are amateurs who have their own radio dishes. Another way to get involved is to help process the radio signals. An ingenious new project called seti@home feeds part of the signal from the giant Arecibo radio telescope to thousands of home computers. When the computer is idle, a program analyzes the data and sends the results back to SETI researchers.

While the SETI program is running, it displays a screensaver that shows the region of sky being analyzed — here Orion — and then any interesting results.

MURMANSK
Russia

WESTERBORK
Netherlands

EFFELSBERG
Germany

GORKY
Russia

KAMCHATKA
Russia

NANÇAY
France

CAUCASUS
Russia

PAMIR
Tajikistan

MEDICINA
Italy

DEEP SPACE STATION
Ukraine

MARS 2
This Russian probe, which was sent into orbit around the Red Planet in 1972, also carried a detector able to pick up pulsed, artificial radio signals.

PROJECT PHOENIX — RISING AGAIN
Researchers lobbied NASA for 30 years to get funding for a SETI program. They were devastated when senators forced NASA to abandon the 10-year project after only one year. Undaunted, the researchers regrouped into a highly visible lobby and began a campaign to attract private funding. Several million dollars poured in — enough to keep the project and personnel afloat for many years to come. Project Phoenix is now managed by Jill Tarter of the SETI Institute.

Project Phoenix's Mobile Research Facility ("murph") can be flown to interface with any radio telescope in the world.

The "murph" is a container van bristling with electronic detection equipment. It can tune in to 28 million frequencies at once.

PERTH
Western Australia

TIDBINBILLA
Australian Capital Territory

PARKES
In 1995, the 210-ft (64-m) radio telescope in New South Wales became the first destination in the southern hemisphere for Project Phoenix's "murph." Although no alien signals were detected, the team improved the sensitivity of their equipment dramatically.

Galactic civilizations

Z
Y
X
W
V
U
T
S

THE FIRST ALIEN MESSAGE we decipher is likely to come from a civilization more advanced than our own. Humans, after all, are the new kids on the cosmic block. Many stars are far older than the Sun, and could have civilizations way ahead of us. It is impossible to know what intelligent life-forms might look like after billions more years of evolution. But scientists predict they will follow similar paths in exploiting energy and information, building vast structures, and perhaps setting up an intergalactic network of communications.

Dyson Sphere

If SETI researchers find a large star giving out lots of infrared heat but little light, they may have located a Dyson Sphere. Made from dismantled planets, the sphere surrounds the star to trap all its energy. Civilizations live on the inside surface of the sphere, with the star always overhead, providing a clean, limitless source of power.

R
Q
P
O
N
M
L
K

Information vs energy

Far-sighted scientists have suggested a scheme for comparing how far alien civilizations have advanced, regardless of how they may look or the nature of their culture. One measure of their progress is controlling energy; another is manipulating information. The graph on this page plots increasing exploitation of energy (left to right, from 0 to 4.4) and processing of information (up the page, from A to Z). Each colored box represents a different combination of information and energy that a civilization could control. We can show Earth's progress to date so far (the solid line), and we would expect our future progress, and that of civilizations ahead of us, to continue on a diagonal path (dashed) of increasing energy and information manipulation.

Blow-up of cross-section through the sphere.

At 1.4 J, a civilization has sufficient energy and information processing to establish regular communications with alien cultures.

At 2.2 L, a civilization can alter its parent star to act as an interstellar beacon.

J
I
H

Our civilization moved sideways (from 0.1 to 0.6) after harnessing the energy of coal, oil, and nuclear power (the Industrial Revolution), then upward (E to H) after it learned to manipulate information with computers (the Information Revolution).

At 0.6 H, Earth is only just on the energy-information graph.

FREEMAN J. DYSON

In 1960, British physicist Freeman Dyson (b.1923) suggested advanced civilizations might surround their stars with artificial habitats — "Dyson Spheres" — to exploit energy to the maximum. Dramatically ahead of his time, he also proposed that humans could genetically modify our bodies to adapt to living in space. Although astronomers have searched for the infrared "heat-energy" signals from Dyson Spheres, none has been found.

Dyson's conventional work spans nuclear and particle physics.

G
F
E
D

Information Revolution

Industrial Revolution

CLASSIFYING CIVILIZATIONS
The idea of ranking civilizations by energy use was devised by Russian scientist Nicolai Kardashev in 1964. A decade later, American astronomer Carl Sagan suggested grading them by their ability to process information as well.

C
B

Type I civilization
Can harness the entire energy of its planet.

A

Information manipulation

Energy manipulation ➡

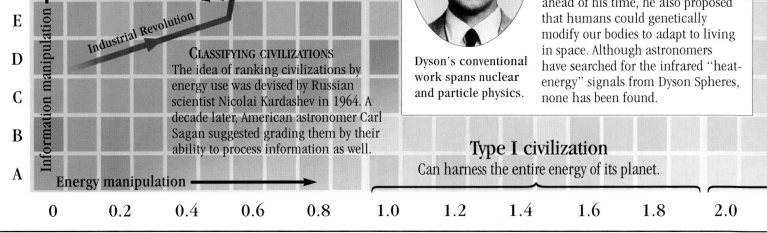

| 0 | 0.2 | 0.4 | 0.6 | 0.8 | 1.0 | 1.2 | 1.4 | 1.6 | 1.8 | 2.0 |

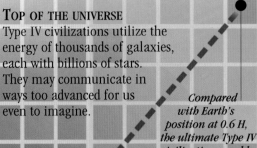

TOP OF THE UNIVERSE
Type IV civilizations utilize the energy of thousands of galaxies, each with billions of stars. They may communicate in ways too advanced for us even to imagine.

Compared with Earth's position at 0.6 H, the ultimate Type IV civilizations could reach 4.4 Z.

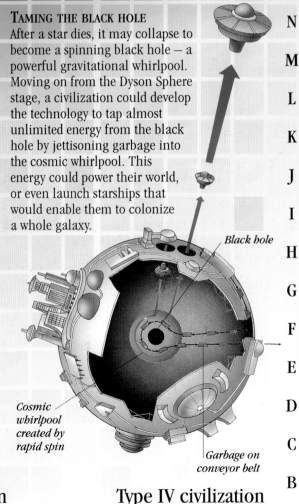

A civilization exploiting a galaxy's energy might look like a quasar — the hot, dazzling core of an active galaxy.

At 3.7 S, a civilization can control the power of a whole galaxy, consisting of billions of individual stars.

At 3.0 O, a civilization can control the mighty gravity of a black hole. Its technology puts it on the threshold of Type III, poised to discover how to harness the power of a whole galaxy.

TAMING THE BLACK HOLE
After a star dies, it may collapse to become a spinning black hole – a powerful gravitational whirlpool. Moving on from the Dyson Sphere stage, a civilization could develop the technology to tap almost unlimited energy from the black hole by jettisoning garbage into the cosmic whirlpool. This energy could power their world, or even launch starships that would enable them to colonize a whole galaxy.

Black hole

At 2.6 M, a civilization can trap the energy of its local star with a Dyson Sphere.

FUTURE GENES
Engineering in the future will take in the microscopic as well as the macroscopic. We are already manipulating the genetic code to grow crops or breed animals with desirable characteristics. We may be able to grow living spare parts to replace those that wear out, and even breed people with bodies adapted to living and traveling in the vacuum of space.

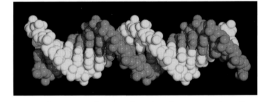

DNA, the complex molecule that contains the genetic code, is the key to controlling our future, when we will be able to process the information in the DNA molecule itself.

Cosmic whirlpool created by rapid spin

Garbage on conveyor belt

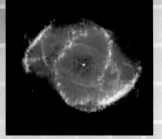

One astronomer argued that the Cat's Eye Nebula was a "beacon" of material dumped from a Type II civilization. But the glowing rings are from a dying star.

| Z |
| Y |
| X |
| W |
| V |
| U |
| T |
| S |
| R |
| Q |
| P |
| O |
| N |
| M |
| L |
| K |
| J |
| I |
| H |
| G |
| F |
| E |
| D |
| C |
| B |
| A |

Type II civilization
Exploits the energy of its star.

Type III civilization
Utilizes the complete energy of its home galaxy.

Type IV civilization
Controls a cluster of galaxies.

| 2.4 | 2.6 | 2.8 | 3.0 | 3.2 | 3.4 | 3.6 | 3.8 | 4.0 | 4.2 | 4.4 |

Ultimate aliens

I N OUR QUEST FOR SIGNS OF ALIEN INTELLIGENCE in the Universe, we may have missed a trick. Perhaps other life-forms might not resemble us in any way, so they also think and behave in ways that are very different. There may even be life-forms out there so extreme or so unexpected that we wouldn't recognize them as living. But what do we mean by "living": how do you define what life is? And when it comes to "intelligence," we encounter the same problem – perhaps some aliens reason so differently from us that communication with them would be an impossibility.

Most spiral galaxies spin much more quickly than expected.

The dark matter in and around a galaxy provides a gravitational pull that keeps the spinning galaxy together.

Spot the alien

We can only guess some of the ways in which alien life could be totally unlike ours. Every image on this page is a kind of "life" that has been proposed at some time by a distinguished scientist. Some may involve different chemistry, adapted to extreme environments. Others may be formless and diffuse, or comprise all the life-forms on one planet as a single huge entity. A few scientists maintain that the Universe itself is alive. Weirdest of all, some aliens may be forever invisible to us, yet passing silently through our bodies every second of the day.

GAIA

The Gaia hypothesis, named after the Greek Earth goddess, maintains that a whole planet can be a living entity. Its plants, animals, atmosphere, and ocean act in concert to preserve a long-term balance. Any individual species upsetting that balance – such as human beings – risks being destroyed.

SILICON LIFE-FORMS

The element silicon combines with other elements in a similar way to carbon, so some scientists have speculated that it could form life. The crystalline, silicon-based life on this airless asteroid organized itself into an intelligent society like a collection of silicon microchips, and can thrive in the vacuum of space and lethal radiation.

The meaning of life

Even scientists cannot agree how to define what life really is. Some say that a living entity uses energy in an orderly way, has a boundary, and can reproduce. Even on Earth, however, that definition isn't watertight, as shown below. When it comes to truly alien environments, perhaps there is no clear distinction between life and non-life.

If a "living entity" has a "boundary, uses energy, and reproduces," then a flame is alive.

If reproduction is essential to life, then the mule – a sterile cross between an ass and a horse – is not alive.

IS THE UNIVERSE ALIVE?

A controversial new theory states that a whole universe can be alive, judged by the idea that life involves success in reproduction. The theory holds that black holes can "bud" whole universes. Those that develop black holes are successful; those that do not are sterile. By a strange quirk of physics, a universe that forms black holes also makes the right chemicals for life like us.

INVISIBLE LIFE?

Studies of spinning galaxies reveal that they are much more massive than they first appear. The extra mass – known as "dark matter" – is invisible and its nature is unknown. Dark matter permeates the whole of the Milky Way and other galaxies, and extends into a large halo that surrounds individual galaxies. If dark matter could build life-forms, they would be invisible and even capable of passing through our bodies without us being aware of them.

Astronomers believe that more than 90% of the Universe consists of invisible, dark matter.

Interstellar clouds are black because they contain dust – "soot" from dying stars. Lit by intense light from a star, the black cloud glows a dull brown.

A black hole in our Universe "buds" a baby universe. This expands and, if it contains black holes, can itself reproduce.

BLACK CLOUDS

Stars are born in dense black clouds of dust and molecules of gas, such as ammonia and carbon dioxide, that emit microwave radiation. In his novel *The Black Cloud*, the astronomer Fred Hoyle imagined that a cloud like this could be intelligent, with molecules communicating by microwaves like nerve cells in a brain. But the cloud needs energy to stay "alive," which means feeding on light from a nearby star – in this case, the Sun. In the book, the repercussions for Earth are not very pleasant.

The Milky Way contains over 5,000 dense dark clouds, each potentially a "Black Cloud" alien.

Starship designer

Bob Forward, who invented "cheelas," is a science fiction writer and was formerly an aerospace engineer with the Hughes Aircraft Corporation. He has designed futuristic spaceships which, if built, could travel to the stars at velocities approaching the speed of light. The spaceships would be vast wire-mesh sails, the size of Texas, propelled along by immensely powerful lasers that stay in orbit around the Sun.

Bob Forward's imaginative designs extend to his famous waistcoats, such as this rainbow one.

CHEELAS

Aside from black holes, neutron stars have the strongest gravity of any object in the Universe. Space engineer Bob Forward has suggested that flattened beings made of the nuclei of atoms – "cheelas" – could live on their searingly hot surfaces. Their life processes depend not on chemistry but on nuclear reactions.

Living on the incandescent surface of a neutron star, cheelas see everything lit from below.

First contact

T HE DAY WE DETECT A SIGNAL from extraterrestrial intelligence will be a turning point in the history of the world. We will know, at last, that we are not alone. The shock waves of the discovery will be felt far beyond the community of SETI scientists. The signal will have an impact on everybody, from heads of government and the world's religious communities through to ordinary individuals – and every group will react in a different way. In the end, there will be two decisions to be made. Should we respond? And, if so, what should we say?

Detection!

Events begin to unfold in 2020 with the detection of an obviously alien signal by Project Phoenix researchers at Greenbank, West Virginia. The signal – called a "carrier wave" – reveals the frequency of the alien broadcast, but it is too weak for any information to be decoded.

CARL SAGAN
Carl Sagan (1934–1996) was one of the most influential proponents of SETI. He was equally comfortable in the fields of astronomy and biology, working on Martian life experiments on the *Viking* missions before becoming a staunch and visionary advocate of SETI. He devised our first messages to the stars sent aboard the *Pioneer* and *Voyager* spacecraft.

Sagan's novel *Contact* gave an illuminating perspective on our reaction to alien signals.

Unidentified signal coming from the constellation Piscis Austrinus, which is picked up by the Greenbank radio telescope

Project Phoenix radio telescope at Greenbank

PROTOCOL
The SETI researchers follow the "Declaration of Principles for Activities Following the Detection of Extraterrestrial Intelligence" – guidelines accepted internationally in 1990.

RELIGIOUS RESPONSE
Religions may be thrown into turmoil when alien intelligence is detected. Most Christians, for example, would worry whether Jesus had also lived and died on these other planets. The Mormon doctrine, though, includes a strong belief in other inhabited worlds.

The Mormon Church is not surprised by the alien signal.

VERIFICATION
One of the protocols in the Declaration of Principles is that the signal must be verified by other teams before it is announced. Several groups of radio astronomers around the world successfully detect the carrier wave. But still no message emerges from the weak signal.

TELLING THE WORLD
The discoverers, having told the relevant professional bodies and the Secretary-General of the United Nations, go public at a press conference. There can be no cover-up: SETI researchers believe in openness.

POLITICAL RESPONSE
At the White House, the US President confirms her commitment to SETI. In order to decode the signal, a huge, very sensitive array of radio telescopes must be built. She promises to fund it – just as President Clinton committed more money to Mars research after a possible Martian microfossil was found in 1996.

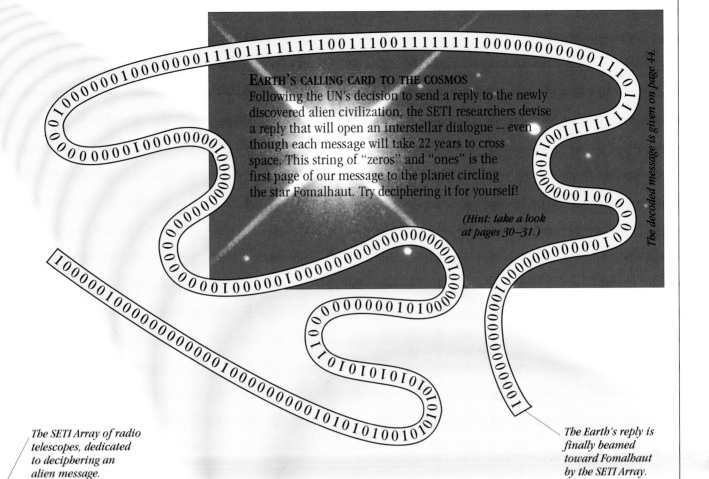

EARTH'S CALLING CARD TO THE COSMOS
Following the UN's decision to send a reply to the newly discovered alien civilization, the SETI researchers devise a reply that will open an interstellar dialogue — even though each message will take 22 years to cross space. This string of "zeros" and "ones" is the first page of our message to the planet circling the star Fomalhaut. Try deciphering it for yourself!

(Hint: take a look at pages 30–31.)

The decoded message is given on page 44.

The SETI Array of radio telescopes, dedicated to deciphering an alien message.

The Earth's reply is finally beamed toward Fomalhaut by the SETI Array.

PUBLIC RESPONSE
The public reacts in a bewildering variety of ways to the news. Some people are euphoric; others feel threatened. The press, at first serious, soon starts to feature alien cartoons, while television cannot show enough old sci-fi movies. Stock markets oscillate wildly as nervous people speculate. A few of the more extreme religious sects commit mass suicide. The military grows cautious. But everyone has been changed, knowing that we have company out there in space.

Stock exchanges react nervously to news of the extraterrestrial signal.

The strangest and most important United Nations debate of all: should we reply to an alien message?

SETI research suddenly becomes a vote winner.

WHAT DOES THE MESSAGE CONTAIN?
Three years later, the powerful SETI Array of radio telescopes is complete. It easily captures the carrier wave, and is powerful enough to reveal within this signal a wealth of complex detail. This is the longed-for message. Experts work on it for months, but only partly succeed in decoding it. The message tells of the language and science of the inhabitants of a planet around the star Fomalhaut, 22 light-years away. But there is much that is indecipherable, to await researchers of the future.

SHOULD WE REPLY?
Now the United Nations is charged with a huge responsibility: should it reply on behalf of the people of Earth? Some experts speak passionately against, arguing that if "they" are hostile, they are close enough on the cosmic scale to travel to Earth and destroy us. But the SETI community convinces the UN that the benefits of contact will outweigh the risks — and are asked to draft a response.

Glossary

ALIEN A form of life not native to the Earth.

AMINO ACID A type of *organic molecule* that forms the building blocks of *protein*.

ASTEROID Small body of rock or metal left over from the building of the *Solar System*. Several have collided with Earth, causing *mass extinctions*.

ATMOSPHERE Mantle of gas surrounding a planet. The mix of gases in the atmosphere, and its density (it must be thick enough), are crucial to the development of life.

ATOMIC NUMBER The number of protons in the nucleus of an atom. Each *element* has a different atomic number.

BALL LIGHTNING Ball-shaped variety of lightning that may be responsible for some sightings of *unidentified flying objects*.

BILLION One thousand million.

BINARY CODE A number system with just two digits – 0 and 1 – used in computers, and for beaming radio messages to potentially inhabited planets.

BLACK HOLE Region of space so dense that its gravity pulls in everything around it, even light. The region around a black hole is crammed with energy, and advanced aliens may be able to utilize this, creating *gravitational waves* that would betray their presence.

CARBON One of the most common *elements* in the Universe. A carbon atom forms bonds – with itself and with other atoms – in more versatile ways than any other element. These carbon molecules form the basis of life on Earth, and are sometimes referred to as *organic molecules*.

CARRIER WAVE The stream of *radio waves* within which is encoded a specific message. Radio messages on Earth are sent on a carrier wave, but domestic radios filter it out, allowing the signal to be heard.

CELL The smallest unit of an organism that can exist. Each cell contains *proteins* and *DNA*.

COMET Leftover debris from the building of the *Solar System*, made largely of ice with a little rock. Comets have bombarded the Earth in the past, leading to *mass extinctions*. Some astronomers believe that comets also provided the bulk of the water that forms Earth's oceans.

DNA DNA, or deoxyribonucleic acid, is present in all *cells*. It makes up chromosomes and holds the crucial genetic blueprint. DNA replicates in an ordered way to transmit genetic information from parent to offspring during reproduction.

ELECTROMAGNETIC NOISE A problem encountered when searching for faint signals of *electromagnetic radiation*,

especially *radio waves*, and caused by interference from other, unwanted signals of similar wavelengths.

ELECTROMAGNETIC RADIATION Radiation made up of electrical and magnetic fields that moves at the speed of light. It ranges from short wavelength gamma rays to long wavelength *radio waves*, taking in X-rays, *ultraviolet radiation*, light, and *infrared radiation*.

ELEMENT A substance that cannot be broken down into anything simpler by means of chemical reactions.

EXTRASOLAR Not belonging to the Sun; beyond the *Solar System*.

EXTRATERRESTRIAL Coming from beyond the Earth.

FLYING SAUCER Popular name for *unidentified flying object*.

G The acceleration felt as the result of the force of gravity acting on a body. Near Earth's surface it is about 9.8 m/s^2 (32 ft/s^2) – defined as 1g. More massive planets have a stronger gravity and therefore higher g forces – their life-forms would be more squashed. On less massive planets, where the gravity is weaker and hence there are low g forces, slender, elongated life-forms would be possible.

GRAVITATIONAL WAVE A ripple in space, which travels at the speed of light, produced by the movement of very massive bodies with high gravity, such as *black holes*.

HABITABLE ZONE The region in a *planetary system*, not too near and not too far from the parent star, where it is possible for life to exist.

HYDROGEN The simplest *element*, the lightest gas, and a very common constituent of many planetary atmospheres.

INFRARED RADIATION Form of *electromagnetic radiation*, with a wavelength between light and microwaves, given out by warm bodies such as planets or artificial structures like Dyson Spheres.

INORGANIC MOLECULE A molecule that does not contain *carbon*.

LASER BEAM An intense beam of light, which could be used to communicate with alien beings far across the Galaxy.

LIGHT-YEAR Distance covered by a ray of light or other *electromagnetic radiation* traveling at 186,000 miles/s (300,000 km/s) in a year. It is about 6.2 million million miles (9.5 million million km).

MASS EXTINCTION An event during which a major proportion of the world's plant and animal species is wiped out, thus affecting the course and evolution of life. There have been several mass extinctions, probably caused by the impacts of *comets* or *asteroids* – although some scientists think that huge outpourings of molten lava were to blame.

METEOR A tiny fragment of dust from *comets* that burns up in the Earth's upper atmosphere, creating a flash. Some have been mistaken for *unidentified flying objects*.

METEORITE A *meteor* large enough to survive the journey through Earth's atmosphere. Large meteorites may have been responsible for *mass extinctions* in the past, although they might also have brought *organic molecules* to our planet – leading to the origin of life.

MICROWAVE *Electromagnetic radiation*, with a wavelength between infrared and radio, emitted by molecules in black, interstellar clouds.

NEUTRINO High-speed, highly penetrating *subatomic particle*. Aliens may use neutrinos for communication.

NEUTRON STAR Collapsed star made largely of *subatomic particles* called neutrons.

ORGANIC MOLECULE A molecule containing the *element carbon*. Organic molecules such as proteins and DNA are the basis of life on Earth.

MESSAGE FROM PLANET EARTH

The message on page 43 contains 247 binary digits (0 or 1), which can be arranged in a pictogram of 19 rows and 13 columns, where 1 appears here as a white square and 0 as a black square. Down the right side is the Solar System – the Sun is six squares wide; the inner planets (Mercury, Venus, Earth and its Moon, and Mars) are single squares; the giant planets (Jupiter, Saturn, Uranus, and Neptune) are two or three squares wide; and tiny Pluto is a single square. The outline human is pointing toward Earth. Below the human are four numbers (1, 6, 7, and 8) in binary code (page 30). These are the atomic numbers for hydrogen, carbon, nitrogen, and oxygen, the most important elements making up the human body.

Index

OZONE LAYER Thin layer of gas in Earth's upper atmosphere, made of ozone – three atoms of oxygen joined together – that absorbs harmful *ultraviolet radiation* from the Sun. The planet Mars, which has no oxygen in its atmosphere, has developed a global "ozone hole," allowing lethal rays to scour its surface.

PERMAFROST Water in a layer just below the surface of the soil that never thaws out, as is the case in the tundra regions on Earth. Much of the water that once flowed on Mars has probably become permafrost.

PLANETARY SYSTEM Family of planets, moons, and leftover debris around a star.

PROTEIN A complex molecule made of *amino acids*. Proteins form most of the structures of living *cells* and control the processes going on inside them.

PULSAR Fast-spinning *neutron star*, a source of natural *radio waves*.

RADIO TELESCOPE Dish or antenna used to detect *radio waves* from space, whether produced by natural or artificial means.

RADIO WAVES *Electromagnetic radiation* with the longest wavelengths, produced by high-speed electrons that can travel unimpeded across the Universe.

SETI Search for extraterrestrial intelligence.

SOLAR SYSTEM The Sun and its family of planets. If used with a lower case "s" (as in solar system), it refers to another star and its planets.

SUBATOMIC PARTICLES The constituents of an atom, such as electrons, protons, and neutrons.

ULTRAVIOLET RADIATION *Electromagnetic radiation* of a short wavelength produced by the Sun and other stars. It damages living *cells* and can wipe out emergent life.

UNIDENTIFIED FLYING OBJECT Phenomenon in the sky that cannot be easily classified.

Acknowledgments

DK would like to thank Lester Cheeseman for additional design work and Amanda Rayner for editorial assistance.

Picture credits: **Camera Press** 42bc, 43br; **Bruce Coleman** 31bra, 31bc; **Colorific/Steve Smith** 42tr; **Corbis UK** 25tc, 37cl; **Dorling Kindersley Picture Library** 12cl, 14br, 31tr, 35tr, 40bc, 40br; **Mary Evans Picture Library** 8tr; **Eye Ubiquitous/ Barry Davies** 42crb; "**Face on Mars**" **Home Page**, internet 16cr; **Fortean Picture Library** 25cl; **Galaxy Picture Library** 26tr, 30cl; **Getty Images** 24bc, 24-25bc; **Ronald Grant Archive** 8bra, 9cla, 9cra, 9blr; **H. Hammel/MIT & NASA** 13bl; **Hencoup Enterprises** 9tl, 28tr, 32tc, 33tr, 34tr, 35btl, 35bc, 41br; /**NASA** 17bl, 19tc; /**NASA/SETI Institute** 34tc; /**RAL** 34cba; **Images Colour Library** 24cl, 24cr, 25br; **Instituto Argentino de Radioastronomia** 34br; **Keystone, Zurich** 26cl; **Kobal Collection** 8cl, 8bl, 8c, 8bcl, 8bcr, 8brb, 9cr, 9crb, 9clb, 9clrb, 9bl, 9bca; **Lowell Observatory** 14tcr, 14cra; **NASA** 34 bcl; **Ohio State University Archives** 33tl; **Rex Features** 42brb

(montage); **San Francisco State University** 26clb; **Science Photo Library** 10bl, 37cr, 39bl; /**Axel Bartel** 43cl; /**Julian Baum** 13cr, 17cr; /**California Association for Research in Astronomy** 13bca; /**John Chumack** 43tr; /**NASA** 16tc, 16cr, 16cl, 30br, 31trb; /**Novosti** 35tlb; /**John Reader** 10br; /**Dr K. Seddon & Dr T. Evans**, Queen's University Belfast 38cb, 39bc; /**Dr Seth Shostak** 30br; /**US Geological Survey** 14cl, 15tr; /**X-Ray Astronomy Group**, Leicester University 39tr; **SETI Institute/Dr Seth Shostak** 34bl; 42cla, 42bl; **South American Pictures** 25cra; **Telegraph Colour Library** 42bra (montage); **Topham Picturepoint** 31cra; **United Nations/Wolf** 31crb; **Universal Pictorial Press & Agency** 12bl

Every effort has been made to trace the copyright holders and we apologize in advance for any unintentional omissions. We would be pleased to insert the appropriate acknowledgment in any subsequent edition of this publication.